Exploring Careers in the MILITARY

Leanne Currie-McGhee

ReferencePoint Press

San Diego, CA

ReferencePoint Press®

Printed in the United States

For more information, contact:
ReferencePoint Press, Inc.
PO Box 27779
San Diego, CA 92198
www.ReferencePointPress.com

LIBRARY OF CONGRESS CATALOGING-IN-PUBLICATION DATA

Names: Currie-McGhee, L. K. (Leanne K.), author.
Title: Exploring careers in the military / by Leanne Currie-McGhee.
Description: San Diego, CA : ReferencePoint Press, Inc., 2024. | Includes bibliographical references and index.
Identifiers: LCCN 2023009822 (print) | LCCN 2023009823 (ebook) | ISBN 9781678205706 (library binding) | ISBN 9781678205713 (ebook)
Subjects: LCSH: United States--Armed Forces--Vocational guidance.
Classification: LCC UB147 .C865 2024 (print) | LCC UB147 (ebook) | DDC 355.002373--dc23/eng/20230413
LC record available at https://lccn.loc.gov/2023009822
LC ebook record available at https://lccn.loc.gov/2023009823

CONTENTS

INTRODUCTION

Something for Everyone

Are you interested in becoming an electrician? Have you considered a career as a doctor? Do you dream about flying an airplane? You can train to become any one of these—and more—while serving in the US military. The air force, army, coast guard, marine corps, navy, and space force make up the US military. Together, they offer opportunities for any number of careers.

Whether in the United States or overseas, military bases, ships, submarines, and field commands are—in some ways—like little cities. They need people trained in dentistry, firefighting, engineering, warehouse management, cooking, and information technology. Others work in mission-specific jobs, such as pilots, explosive ordnance disposal technicians, and infantry soldiers. Approximately 80 percent of military personnel who fill these roles are enlisted. Enlisted personnel are required to have a high school diploma or general equivalency diploma to enter. The other 20 percent are officers, who must be college graduates.

In recent years all branches have struggled to meet their personnel recruitment goals. For this reason, the branches are offering recruits more flexible contracts. This includes two-year commitments as opposed to the typical four- or six-year commitments, greater say in first duty stations, and sign-on bonuses.

Many Perks

A major benefit of serving in the military is the opportunity to see the world and experience adventures not available in most civilian careers. As a child growing up in Burke, Virginia, Madeline Swegle saw the Blue Angels, the navy's flight demonstration squadron that performs aerial displays across the nation. She knew almost immediately that she too wanted to pilot a jet. In 2020—after graduating from the US Naval Academy, receiving an officer commission, and undergoing pilot training—she fulfilled her dream: Swegle became the first Black woman to become a tactical jet pilot in the US Navy. Recalling the first time she piloted a jet, Swegle says, "It was crazy to be in such a higher performance aircraft. I was really excited on takeoff, feeling the acceleration and getting thrown back in the seat. . . . It's fun because it's difficult."[1]

Although experiences like this are part of the military, there are practical benefits too. Among the practical benefits are job security and a steady paycheck. Other such benefits include free medical care for military personnel and their families and either free housing or a housing allowance. Career advancement is also possible, both for enlisted personnel and officers. Advancement is typically determined by time in service, types of tours served, tests and certifications, and evaluations. Those who advance in the ranks take on more responsibilities and receive higher pay.

FACT
The US armed forces had 1.3 million active-duty personnel in 2022.

For some individuals, military service brings life-changing results. Aleda Leaks enlisted in the army at age seventeen. She credits the army with changing her life. She grew up in a poor and crime-ridden area of Memphis, Tennessee. She saw the army as a chance to start a new life. In 2021, two years after entering the army, she had earned an associate's degree in information technology as well as industry certifications. She had also managed to save enough money to buy a car and, with help

Sample Military Pay Scales, 2023

Basic pay for military personnel, whether enlisted or officers, is based on years of service and rank. The person's rank usually corresponds with his or her pay grade. Individuals with more years of service and higher rank achieve higher pay grades. As in the civilian world, basic pay is subject to taxes. Some military personnel supplement their income with allowances for housing, clothing, and other needs. Special and incentive pays, such as for hardship duty, can also increase income.

A Sample of Monthly Active-Duty Enlisted Pay Scale for 2023 (all branches)

Sample Pay Grades	Years of Service: <2	2	3	4	6	8	10
E-2	$2,149.24	$2,149.24	$2,149.24	$2,149.24	$2,149.24	$2,149.24	$2,149.24
E-3	$2,260.10	$2,402.22	$2,547.89	$2,547.89	$2,547.89	$2,547.89	$2,547.89
E-4	$2,503.41	$2,631.67	$2,774.12	$2,914.95	$3,039.03	$3,039.03	$3,039.03
E-5	$2,730.29	$2,914.31	$3,055.15	$3,199.20	$3,423.82	$3,658.44	$3,851.48
E-6	$2,980.38	$3,279.76	$3,424.79	$3,565.30	$3,711.94	$4,041.94	$4,171.18
E-7	$3,445.74	$3,760.92	$3,905.30	$4,095.44	$4,244.66	$4,500.54	$4,644.92

A Sample of Monthly Active-Duty Officer Pay Scale for 2023 (all branches)

Sample Pay Grades	Years of Service: <2	2	3	4	6	8	10
O-1	$3,637.17	$3,786.06	$4,576.92	$4,576.92	$4,576.92	$4,576.92	$4,576.92
O-2	$4,190.83	$4,772.53	$5,496.68	$5,682.64	$5,799.30	$5,799.30	$5,799.30
O-3	$4,849.88	$5,497.65	$5,933.36	$6,469.95	$6,780.30	$7,120.29	$7,340.09
O-4	$5,516.34	$6,385.19	$6,811.88	$6,906.30	$7,301.73	$7,726.16	$8,254.69
O-5	$6,393.25	$7,202.15	$7,700.38	$7,794.16	$8,105.80	$8,291.43	$8,700.71
O-6	$7,669.13	$8,425.17	$8,978.19	$8,978.19	$9,012.67	$9,398.76	$9,450.00

E = Enlisted **O** = Officer

Source: Brittany Crocker and Ryan Guina, "2023 Military Pay Charts," The Military Wallet, January 24, 2023. https://themilitarywallet.com.

from a low-interest housing loan for active-duty military personnel and veterans, a house. She works as an army information technology specialist and says, "I go to work every day with a smile on my face."[2] For Leaks, the army opened up a life she had only dreamed about.

Military Life Can Also Mean Sacrifices

While serving in the military has many benefits, it is important to remember that military service can also require sacrifices. Often, a military career comes with being deployed away from family for months at a time. And you must go to the duty that you are assigned, even if it is not your first choice. You cannot quit the military until you have fulfilled your service contract, which is from two to six years. And no matter which job an individual does in the military, he or she will always have additional duties. These may include mandatory physical fitness, standing watch, or cleaning the barracks. Lastly, there is always the possibility of being in a dangerous situation—in combat or in any number of other scenarios.

> **FACT**
> The US Space Force, the newest and smallest branch of the US military, was established in 2019.

Still, the opportunities offered by military service make it a worthwhile path for many individuals. Davis Jkwon joined the army in 2018 and says it changed him into a hard worker with a strong work ethic. He works as an army human resources specialist. As part of that job, he prepares personnel documents, maintains soldiers' service records, manages soldiers' identification cards and tags, and performs other related tasks. Jkwon says, "If you want to be a better you, this is the place to be."[3]

CHAPTER ONE

Skilled Trades Careers

Whether fixing a jeep during a field exercise, servicing an engine of a fighter jet, or repairing a leak in a barracks bathroom, military personnel in the skilled trades do the work that keeps the commands running. Every military base—whether overseas or in the United States—and nearly every other location where military personnel live and work rely on construction workers, electricians, plumbers, mechanics, welders, painters, equipment operators, and more.

Military jobs in the skilled trades often look a lot like the same jobs in civilian life, but not always. In the military, skilled trades can involve work in settings or on equipment that specifically meets the needs of the armed forces. This is the case for aviation machinist mate Elisa Morales, who joined the navy right after graduating from high school. She is assigned to the Helicopter Sea Combat Squadron on the USS *Charleston*, whose home port is San Diego, California. Her job is to keep the helicopters assigned to the ship working. "Basically, I'm a mechanic, but for helicopters. I inspect, repair, and maintain the engines, rotor systems and fuel systems of the helicopter on board. I'm most proud to see everyone return from their flight," says Morales. "I just want to see my team get back safe and into their beds every night."[4]

Whereas Morales is on a ship, other personnel working in the skilled trades are on bases. Often, these jobs require work in areas that are mission critical, jobs that are intrinsic to waging war. As an example, while based in the desert at Al Dhafra Air Base in the United Arab Emirates, Nicholas Mannion, an air force heating, ventilation, and air-conditioning (HVAC) journeyman, works in the 110°F (43.3°C) heat to keep the air-conditioning running. "The gratitude expressed by sweaty customers after we fix their unit always makes me and my team feel prideful," Mannion says. "But there are many prideful instances where we've fixed the A/C [air-conditioning] for heat-sensitive equipment, whether that be the servers at the communications squadron or the control rooms for the [unmanned aerial vehicles]."[5] Morales, Mannion, and others in the skilled trades use their skills to keep the military ready for action.

Education and Training

All enlisted personnel must pass a physical and have their high school diploma or general equivalency diploma in order to enter any service. Once in the military, no matter what branch, these personnel go through basic training, also known as boot camp. In boot camp, which lasts seven to fourteen weeks, enlistees undergo physical training, combat training, and learn the basics of weaponry, and the essentials of military life.

After boot camp, service personnel receive more training in the field they are assigned to. Their assignment is initially based on the preferences they gave their recruiter and how they did on the Armed Services Vocational Aptitude Battery (ASVAB). The ASVAB is a timed aptitude test of multiple types of skills, such as mathematics, mechanical knowledge, and reading. Length of training varies by assignment. Someone who has been assigned the occupation specialty of construction mechanic in the navy will attend sixteen weeks of specific training in all areas of construction at Port Hueneme, California. Meanwhile, an electrician systems

FACT
The military spent over $10 billion on the construction and management of military facilities in 2021.

specialist in the air force will attend Sheppard Air Force Base in Texas for ninety-nine days to complete the technical training needed to work as an electrician.

In certain specialties, such as anything involving nuclear power, the training is longer and more intensive. Machinist mates who work on nuclear-powered ships operate and maintain steam turbines and gears that are part of the ship's propulsion machinery. After boot camp, also known as basic school, the individuals who do this job report to A-School in Charleston, South Carolina. The six-month course includes classes in trigonometry and power distribution, among other subjects. Then they attend the navy's Nuclear Power School, also in Charleston, where they study nuclear physics and reactor engineering. Next they attend prototype training, which is training with a simulated power unit, at the Nuclear Power Training Unit in either Charleston or Ballston Spa, New York. Over the course of six

Army mechanics do maintenance on a Humvee at a worksite in Belgium. Mechanics, electricians, construction workers, plumbers, welders, and equipment operators are among the many military personnel who work in the skilled trades.

More than a Hobby

"The army did more than turn my hobby into a career—it turned it more into a very interesting adventure. . . . Just before I joined the military, I took up a hobby and repaired my mom and dad's vehicles. My dad was teaching me. I worked at different odd jobs . . . the army gave me meaning in life, more meaning than I could expect. I have done more in the army than I have ever done before the army."

—Elliot Johnston, US Army wheeled vehicle mechanic

Quoted in Go Army, *Repairing Army Vehicles as a 91B*, YouTube, 2022. www.youtube.com/watch?v=EoHnxGKPz14.

months, they learn the fundamentals of a naval nuclear power plant and the mechanical, electrical, and reactor subsystems. One machinist mate who completed the nuclear training says, "In school they teach the very basics, I kid you not, adding and subtracting to nuclear theory. It's hard and not everyone can do it, but a lot of people that didn't think they could do it, have been able to do it."[6]

On the Job

Regardless of which trade someone works in, his or her job nearly always involves some type of construction, maintenance, or repairs. An electrician, for example, might be called on to fix an electrical short in a hospital. Or that electrician might be tasked with wiring a new building. An individual's duties also are dependent on his or her experience and time in the military. As a senior chief, navy machinery repairman Tarah Horney has risen to a high level in the enlisted ranks. After initially joining the navy, she served on a *Nimitz*-class aircraft carrier for five years, with the job of maintenance and repairs. Ten years and several duty stations later, she was assigned to the *Arleigh Burke*–class guided-missile destroyer USS *Carney*, stationed in Rota, Spain, when not at sea. On the *Carney*, Horney's job is to coordinate, schedule, conduct, and document maintenance on equipment and machines throughout

A Bit of Everything

"I work with anything water flows through basically, so water fountains, toilets, showers. We go around different places at the base and collect different [water] samples from different locations to make sure the water has decent chlorine levels to make it safe for our personnel to use. We usually do digs to install new things or repair things that are broken. There might be a water line break and sometimes we dig for sewage line breaks. We also do fuel systems . . . to maintain the integrity of fuel systems for our jets and planes."

—Nyraysha Benjamin, US Air Force water and fuel systems maintenance specialist

Quoted in US Air Force Recruiting, *Getting Our Airmen Clean Water: Water and Fuel System Maintenance Specialist Nyraysha Benjamin*, YouTube, 2022. www.youtube.com/watch?v=3UGAdSq8sHk.

the ship. Additionally, she provides training, both formal and informal, to the sailors on how to accomplish these tasks. This duty combines her knowledge of machinery maintenance and repair with management capabilities. "I work hard to stay knowledgeable, both with my primary duties and general Navy information because I can't train or guide my Sailors if I am not an expert in my field or in the Navy as an organization," Horney says. "The day Sailors stop asking me questions or stop asking for advice, is probably the day I need to hang it up for good."[7]

Ayelech Bushnell also works in a skilled trade. She is a navy construction electrician. In 2022 Bushnell was assigned to an exercise in the Arctic Ocean. The job was to build and equip a navy encampment complete with command center, barracks, cafeteria, bathrooms, wireless internet, and a 2,500-foot-long (762 m) runway. All of this had to be built on a large, floating chunk of ice, and it had to be able to withstand the severe Arctic climate. The job included installation of plumbing, HVAC, and electrical equipment. Bushnell and ten other members of the navy construction battalion unit known as Seabees spent three weeks on the project.

Working Conditions

Working conditions for military personnel in the skilled trades depend on the assignment, service branch, and duty station. The Arctic project that Bushnell worked on required that she work long hours, both day and night, in extremely cold temperatures. Other service members who work in the skilled trades do most of their work indoors, but even then they might have to deal with extreme temperatures. Fixing a broken air-conditioning unit might mean working indoors, but it also might require working in a small, hot, cramped space until the repairs are complete. Working conditions on a ship or submarine also vary. Engine rooms tend to be hot. Rooms that house weapons or computer equipment tend to be cold. And often, skilled trades personnel on a ship or submarine work in tight spaces. The work they do often requires a lot of standing, walking, crouching, or sometimes even lying on the floor.

FACT

As of March 2022, approximately 334,000 military service personnel served in skilled trade fields, according to the US Department of Defense's Defense Manpower Data Center.

Finding a Good Fit

As with any career field, certain characteristics make for a better fit in the skilled trades. Anyone who works in a skilled trade has to be detail oriented. Precision matters when installing or fixing equipment or running or testing machinery. Another key trait is to be a problem solver. Power goes out. Heating systems break. Machines will not start. It is the skilled tradesperson who must assess the situation, determine the problem, and decide the best route to fix these problems. Lastly, a person in this type of field needs to be thorough. Continued maintenance of vehicles, operational checks on generators, and adherence to testing of mechanical tools are all necessary for the jobs to be completed well. People who like to work with their hands also tend to do well in the skilled trades, as do those who enjoy learning and understanding how things work.

Job Prospects in the Civilian World

People with backgrounds in the skilled trades are in high demand in the civilian world. By late 2021 nearly 1 million manufacturing jobs, such as welders and machinists, were unfilled, according to a study published by the Manufacturing Institute and the global professional services network Deloitte. This is likely to mean many job options for military personnel who have worked in skilled trades. Construction workers, plumbers, electricians, utilities workers, appliance repair people, and mechanics who trained and worked in the military are likely to have success in finding equivalent or similar civilian jobs. The federal government and many companies have programs that help match veterans transitioning to civilian careers with those jobs.

CHAPTER TWO

Service Careers

The military could not complete its work without all of the personnel who provide essential support for service members, daily operations, long-term missions, and more. Both officers and enlisted personnel can serve in military service careers. Regardless of rank, these individuals keep the military functioning day in and day out. They provide services ranging from contracting with suppliers to providing equipment for helicopters to handling payroll and accounting to working with the news media to making sure active-duty personnel have healthy meals every day.

Navy culinary specialist Fiona Puno serves on the ship USS *Truxtun*, a guided-missile destroyer. From early morning to evening, Puno works in the kitchen to make meals, along with the kitchen crew, for the hundreds that serve on the ship. In 2022 Puno designed a chocolate and vanilla cake decorated with cherries and chocolate chips for a ceremony aboard the *Truxtun*. Her cake received much praise from the crew and the ship's commanding officer. Responses like these keep Puno excited about her service in the navy. "My hobby became my job," says Puno. "I just want to make people happy and show them that there is still love in the world."[8]

Working as a cook is just one of the many service careers in the military. Another important area is supply—supply officers and enlisted personnel ensure parts are available for ships, helicopters, and other heavy vehicles and equipment. They make sure military kitchens are well stocked with food and that military hospitals and medical units have the supplies and equipment they need for emergencies and everyday health concerns. As the lead supply officer at Naval Medical Center Portsmouth in 2020, Stanley Favard ensured that the command had all of the medical supplies and biomedical and maintenance equipment the hospital needed to function. When COVID-19 became a global pandemic, Favard and his team then needed to acquire large numbers of items like face masks, hand sanitizer, face shields, and disinfectants. "As you know, at one point in time, there was a (nationwide) shortage of critical supplies," says Favard. "We took on extended hours and worked with manufacturers in order to ensure the hospital had everything it needed for our staff and patients."[9] With Favard and others in military service careers, the military branches can smoothly run their operations.

Education and Training

As with nearly all military officers, in order to receive a commission as an officer, those in a military service career must have a college degree and pass a physical. Certain officers in the service careers have additional requirements or preferences. For example, a STEM or business degree is required for supply officers,

Millions of Meals

"Navy culinary specialists feed on average more than 78 million wholesome and nutritious meals per year, supporting 294 galleys afloat and ashore. Their unwavering support of the Navy . . . ensures our fighting forces operate at peak performance, ready to respond to threats worldwide. Our culinary professionals are the backbone of Sailor readiness; nothing impacts Sailors on a day-to-day basis more than the food our Culinary Specialists prepare for them."

—Leanne Riley, US Navy food service director

Quoted in DVIDS, "Navy Culinary Specialists Continue Turkey Day Traditions," November 22, 2021. www.dvidshub.net.

a communications or journalism degree is preferred in public affairs, and to be a judge advocate general (JAG) officer, or navy lawyer, you must have either graduated from or be attending law school. Once in the military, service career officers will attend specialty training for their particular career and branch. Navy JAG officers attend Naval Justice School, a ten-week course that focuses on the basics of military justice, investigations, and national security law. Chaplains, who are also considered service personnel, get special training too. In the army, they attend a sixty-four-day Chaplain Basic Officer Leader Course in Fort Jackson, South Carolina. The course focuses on physical fitness, leadership, and spiritual growth.

> **FACT**
> The Uniform Code of Military Justice is the main legal code that applies to all members of the US military—and it is essential knowledge for JAG officers.

Enlisted personnel in nearly all fields begin their training with boot camp. Once that training is complete, they also get specialized training for whichever job they will be doing. Navy mass communication specialists work in public affairs on news, media, and websites, reporting military information to service personnel and the civilian world. Mass communication specialists attend A-School at Fort George G. Meade in Maryland to learn how to take still and digital photography and how to write news articles, news releases, and the like. Meanwhile, army human resources specialists, who perform administrative duties such as filing and paperwork, attend a nine-week school where they learn to use office software, prepare reports and requests, and gain an understanding of personnel records.

On the Job

Service jobs in the military are similar to service jobs in the civilian world, but there are differences. Drew McGinley is a chaplain in the army. When he works on base, his days start with physical training. Every morning he and his squad run 3 miles (4.8 km) with rucksacks on their backs. Throughout the day he attends

In the mess decks of an aircraft carrier, a Navy culinary specialist ices cupcakes in preparation for a celebration. Personnel in military service careers perform a wide range of jobs including cooking, payroll and accounting, supply chain, and public affairs.

meetings with other chaplains, setting up services of several religions and ministry events for the soldiers. His day also includes time in the office, where he counsels soldiers and/or their family members. He also sets aside time to connect with soldiers on the base so they know who he is and that he is available anytime they need or want to talk. Attending battalion events and even taking part in field exercises offer other ways for him to connect with the soldiers. "As a chaplain, you try to make the most of the time you have so that way you can be with soldiers and meet them and their needs where they're at while they're doing their jobs,"[10] McGinley says.

FACT
As of 2020 there were over twenty-eight hundred chaplains serving in the US military, representing several religions.

Other military service personnel work at jobs that can also be found in the civilian world, but as with chaplains, there are some key differences. Retail sales specialists, for instance, run stores for military personnel. Stores on military bases are not much different from other stores. But some stores are on ships. Rafael Gonzalez is a retail specialist on the guided-missile destroyer USS *Roosevelt*. His job as store manager entails stocking shelves, helping customers, tracking inventory, and supervising other retail specialists at the ship store. A unique aspect of this job on a ship is that Gonzalez has to determine what the sailors want and need, then order and stock these items while in port before going back to sea. While at sea, ship's store specialists often work around the clock in order to be able to provide sailors on duty with needed items.

Working Conditions

Service personnel can be assigned anywhere the military operates. For instance, a JAG could be assigned to a ship. A logistics specialist could be working in temporary facilities out in the field during an infantry training exercise. Bases in the United States and overseas also require any number of service personnel. Depending on the job, they might work in a warehouse, in a kitchen, in a store, or in an office setting.

While on bases, many of these jobs have regular working hours, but there may be night and weekend duty. If the military is short on people to fulfill duties, those who are there must cover the jobs. "We've had a few challenges, but we tackled them head

Many Hats

"A public affairs specialist has many different roles. We have our photographers, our videographers, and . . . we go out in the field and shoot training exercises, we do stand up interviews . . . [and] we do the podcast in the studio. . . . There is a lot that goes into public affairs that a lot of people don't know."

—Chelsea Baker, Army National Guard public affairs specialist

Quoted in SC National Guard, *A Day in the Life of a Public Affairs Specialist with the South Carolina National Guard*, YouTube, 2021. www.youtube.com/watch?v=dK1-6LTkoOY.

on," says navy supply officer Favard regarding his time during the COVID-19 pandemic at Naval Medical Center Portsmouth. "We had to begin to cross-train, work different shifts, and meet the same demand with fewer people. This has really tested our capabilities but despite minor setbacks, we've been able to handle any request that comes across our desk."[11]

Finding a Good Fit

People who work in service careers in the military largely work behind the scenes. They need to be comfortable with the idea that although their jobs are less visible than some, they and their colleagues in all the different career fields help keep the military running.

Many service-related jobs require good communications skills. Retail specialists and supply personnel deal with customers throughout the day. Chaplains, finance officers, security specialists, JAG personnel, communication specialists, and culinary specialists all deal with people often, so it is necessary to be able to express their ideas both orally and in writing and also to listen carefully to others.

Job Prospects in the Civilian World

Most of the service career jobs have counterparts in the civilian world. Financial officers, JAG officers, and supply officers have the opportunity to find high-paying professional jobs as accountants, lawyers, and supply chain or inventory managers. Enlisted personnel who have training in culinary, finance, security, or retail will be able to look for comparable jobs working in restaurants, accounting firms, police departments, and different types of stores.

Many companies value the leadership skills and responsibilities that come with military service. That plus the training and experience in any number of service jobs is likely to open many doors to job opportunities in civilian life.

CHAPTER THREE

Intelligence and Cybersecurity Careers

Cyberwarfare has become a new frontier for the military. It involves protecting the United States and its allies from a growing number of cyberattacks and actively targeting adversaries who carry out those attacks. Accomplishing this mission requires cyberwarfare personnel who can detect, analyze, and neutralize the threats. Military members who work in this field have titles such as cyberwarfare officer, cyberoperations specialist, and cyberoperations officer. Steffan Hinkle chose the army and the job of cyberoperations specialist because of his personal interests and because he feels it will continue to gain in importance. This job, he explains, "was a clear choice, as I had always worked a lot with computers and developed a passion for it. Over time everything will continue moving online, and the cyber domain will become more and more crucial."[12]

Another area that requires people with the ability to identify and analyze threats is intelligence. Personnel in military intelligence obtain all sorts of data and analyze it. They might be tasked with tracking the activities of allies or adversaries. They are also always looking for potential threats, and when they identify a threat, they relay that information to those in

Reaching the President

"While we were doing our mission . . . we picked up [information] and relayed it back to our command. It went all the way up the chain to the president very quickly . . . we picked up this intelligence and it was shot back all the way. That was rewarding."

—Dennis Wischmeier, US Navy intelligence officer

Quoted in Today's Military "Dennis Wischmeier," 2023. www.todaysmilitary.com.

command. They obtain that information with the help of computers, satellite imagery, and interactions with people on the ground in locations around the world. The intelligence field also includes cryptologists—people who decipher encoded transmissions from groups and countries that represent a threat to the United States and its allies. Military members who work in intelligence have titles such as cryptology specialist, intelligence analyst, and intelligence officer.

Education and Training

There is a high bar for entry into military intelligence and cyber careers. For enlisted personnel, ASVAB scores must be high overall, particularly in arithmetical reasoning for cyber careers and verbal expression and paragraph comprehension for intelligence work. For enlisted personnel the path to jobs in intelligence includes advanced schooling, such as a thirteen-week course in Dam Neck, Virginia, in the navy, where they study subjects such as data analysis, information gathering, using intelligence equipment, topography, and briefing skills. For cyber fields, the training typically is around fifteen to forty-five weeks, depending on the specific job and military branch. In the air force, most enlisted personnel in cyber fields attend cyber school at Keesler Air Force Base in Mississippi and learn about networks, databases, operation systems, viruses, and cyber laws. Throughout their training, many in the enlisted cyber careers attend military classes in which they earn certifications that are also applicable in the civilian world.

For cyber officers, a STEM degree is preferred by the branches, while intelligence officers should have a STEM, political science, or international relations degree. The navy requires a bachelor's degree in computer science or computer engineering to be a cyberwarfare engineer and a science or mathematics degree to be a cryptologic warfare officer. Because all of these careers require high-level security clearances, a candidate's background will be closely analyzed to ensure he or she can obtain the necessary security clearance, which is typically a top secret clearance. All intelligence officers attend specialty school for five to six months, depending on the branch. For example, army intelligence officers spend six months in military intelligence school at Fort Huachuca in Arizona. They cover subjects like how to develop an accurate intelligence analysis report, lead intelligence projects, and integrate intelligence information with combat operations. Cyber officers in all service branches attend courses lasting nine weeks or more at locations that include Maxwell-Gunter Air Force Base in Alabama for the air force and Fort Gordon in Georgia for the army. In these courses they learn about networks, cyberthreat assessment, and exploitation techniques (that is, how to use cybertechnology to capture confidential information from adversaries).

FACT
The US Cyber Command was created in 2010 to defend and counter threats to defense systems and the nation's critical infrastructure.

On the Job

People who work in military intelligence collect all sorts of data. This includes weather data that could affect exercises or missions, data on the movements of adversaries and allies, data on the location of weapons and troops, and more. They analyze this data to understand what is happening, then create intelligence briefings and present them in oral and/or written form to higher-ranking military officials for decision-making. Navy intelligence specialist Amanda Shears has served in intelligence for almost ten years, much of the time with aviation squadrons. One of her tours was with a patrol squadron that protects the navy fleet at sea. Her job there was to provide briefings detailing the location of adversaries (known as red forces) that might be encountered during flights. "I was with the P8 [a surveillance and patrol plane] squadron, giving them intel briefs, letting them know what the situational awareness picture is when they were going into their operating area . . . where [red forces are] positioned, and what their standoff is . . . which is how far away we have to be so they can't attack us."[13]

Those in cyber careers defend US networks and/or take the offensive to disrupt adversarial countries' or terrorist groups' networks. They might spend their days scanning various networks,

A Space Force member works on a computer at a military base in California. Military intelligence and cybersecurity personnel rely on computers and satellite imagery for gathering and analyzing certain types of information.

checking for breaches, setting up new security systems, testing existing security systems for vulnerabilities, and researching the latest technologies in their field. Air force cyber surety specialist Jacob Morgan describes his job with the 182nd Communications Flight, an airlift wing in Illinois: "It's our job to . . . make sure we have the best and most up-to-date things protecting our information," he says. "You stay up-to-date on all the latest technologies, all the latest attacks that are happening, how to prevent them. Personally, I love my job."[14]

FACT
The three security clearance levels military people may be approved to hold are confidential, secret, and top secret.

Working Conditions

Intelligence officers and specialists can be assigned at commands around the world. They work on bases, in the field, and on aircraft, ships, and subs. They might even have to parachute out of aircraft if they are assigned to work with a special operations team. "You could be in the day to day, jumping out of aircraft to supporting special operations. Or you could be working back in the United States sitting behind the desk 9 to 5. And everywhere and everything in between," explains Reed Gann, an air force intelligence officer. "And that diversity is one of the things I enjoy the most."[15] Whether intelligence personnel work indoors or outdoors, and how closely they work with other people, depends on their duty station and the information they are asked to collect and analyze. Plus, not all intelligence is gathered by computers or satellites. For example, someone who works in intelligence in the army might spend his or her day talking to local residents of a village near a combat zone. An air force intelligence specialist might work in a command center reviewing satellite images, computer data, and patterns of ship or aircraft movements.

Most individuals in the cyber and cryptologic fields work indoors, sitting in air-conditioned spaces and working on computers. They can be in cyber command centers or assigned to squadrons, ships, or submarines. Those on bases usually work daytime hours, but sometimes they also have to work nights or weekends. The tempo of the work depends on the duty station and tasks. At times cyber and cryptologic personnel may be assigned to a command where they perform routine maintenance on networks and servers. Other times they could be called on to deal with emergencies or active threats to military computer systems.

Finding a Good Fit

Cyber and intelligence fields both require people with high-level analytical, problem-solving, and investigative skills. People who like and are skilled at puzzles and logic problems, in addition to being mathematically inclined, often do well in these fields. They also must be able to analyze information and decide what route to take to deal with the situation they have analyzed. They must be able to constantly learn new technologies and keep up with the latest threats.

Those in intelligence fields need to be effective at communicating both orally and in written form, since they often give reports to higher-level officers. They must be able to clearly and succinctly explain what is happening and then answer any questions. Because their information may be needed at the highest levels, they must be confident and self-assured when presenting information.

Job Prospects in the Civilian World

Those who choose to leave the military usually find themselves with multiple opportunities. Cyber is a large and growing field in the civilian world. Many companies will pay well for personnel with certifications obtained through military service. Companies large and small, as well as government agencies, seek those with

Gathering Info

"We're responsible for your interrogations, your strategic debriefings, and your military source operations. The skills we train on [are] advanced people skills. You're working on questioning, and you're working a lot on human psychology."

—John Gilliam, US Army human intelligence collector

Quoted in US Army, *So, You Want to Be a Human Intelligence Collector?*, YouTube, 2022. www.youtube.com/watch?v=FlhliVGhxK0.

cyber experience for jobs such as cyber systems analysts, network administrators, database analysts, and risk-management analysts. Intelligence careers can lead to jobs in the Central Intelligence Agency, Federal Bureau of Investigation, and National Security Agency. These jobs include investigators, political analysts, and weapons analysts. High security clearances, technical knowledge, and certifications can lead to lucrative and satisfying civilian careers.

CHAPTER FOUR

Medical Careers

Medical careers in the military are wide ranging, and people who can do these jobs are always in demand. The medical professions in the military mirror those found in civilian life. They include nurses, doctors, pharmacists, dentists, physical therapists, dieticians, occupational therapists, psychologists, dental hygienists, and a wide array of support staff. Any of the medical careers that would be found in a civilian hospital or health clinic are also found in the military.

What is more, members of the military who work in the medical professions are stationed at locations worldwide. They work just about anywhere that has any kind of US military presence. For example, Richard Martinez is an army pharmacy technician stationed at Landstuhl Regional Medical Center in Germany. He describes his job this way:

> Every day, we make sure we have the proper medications needed. If (a new medication) is needed, we'll find it and make sure we have it for those warfighters coming here from downrange. It's always something new every day. I interact with every department, clinic and ward throughout the hospital. It's actually very rewarding being able to give people what they want and what they need.[16]

While many people in the medical professions work in traditional clinics or hospitals, others are trained to provide care in the field and in active war zones. Combat medics, medical corpsmen, flight nurses, field nurses, and others are specifically trained to work with units in the field and to provide medical care under extreme conditions. They learn how to provide immediate care with limited resources while under fire.

FACT
The Military Health System includes more than 51 hospitals, 424 clinics, 248 dental clinics, and 251 veterinary facilities in the United States and around the world.

Medical careers in the military also include personnel who work with animals that perform duties for the military. Veterinarians and veterinary technicians care for military working dogs, dolphins, sea lions, horses, and mules. Dogs work in areas such as explosives detection, search and rescue, and security patrols. Dolphins and sea lions work in the US Navy Marine Mammal System to help keep ports secure. In some settings, the army uses horses and mules for transport and patrols.

Education and Training

Many medical personnel such as nurses, physicians, and dentists complete their education and obtain any needed certifications or licensing before joining the military. Once they enter the military, they attend officer training school. Once that training is complete, they are immediately placed in roles in their fields. However, the military branches also offer special scholarships for people who wish to serve in these positions and are accepted to or enrolled in medical, dental, and nursing programs. If accepted by the medical scholarship program, the military pays for their additional schooling; in exchange, they agree to serve for a set amount of time—usually two years for every year of schooling paid for by the military.

Enlisted personnel who want to serve in medical roles must first qualify through their ASVAB scores, and generally, higher scores in science, mathematical knowledge, and comprehension sections are required. If accepted for a role such as a psychological operations specialist, practical nursing specialist, or dental specialist, the individual attends advanced training with his or her branch of the military. Training for medical fields is often longer and more intense than for many other military areas. For example, nursing specialists in the army attend 52 weeks of Advanced Individual Training at Fort Sam Houston in Texas, and air force diagnostic imaging technicians also attend training at Fort Sam Houston for 340 to 450 days.

On the Job

Often medical personnel are stationed at military health clinics and hospitals, which can be in the United States or overseas. Their jobs are similar to their civilian counterparts who do surgeries, physical exams, dental work, laboratory work, and more. For example, military and civilian radiologic technologists perform various types of imaging, including X-rays, computed tomography scans, and magnetic resonance imaging. The patients may be service members, veterans, or their families. One army radiologic specialist who is stationed at Fort Sill in Oklahoma, says most of his patients are veterans who seek care at the base clinic and hospital. He describes a typical day with his crew:

> So, we get up for [physical training] about 0530 [5:30 a.m.]. We go to the gym, work out with our fellow soldiers, even our civilians sometimes. We go out on runs. We have certain walks and parades we do. Then we come into the actual hospital, Reynolds Army Health Clinic. We go ahead and turn on the machines for those exams, whether they be chest X-rays, or it could be for their feet, legs, hips or skull. Make sure everything is good for our patients.[17]

Other medical service personnel perform their medical jobs alongside critical warfighting duties. A navy special amphibious reconnaissance corpsman (SARC) has the job of providing medical care to a marine platoon while also serving as a sharpshooter in combat situations. "The most unique quality about being a SARC is

In the Fight

"One thing that's interesting about Navy Corpsman history is that there are more Corpsmen who have received the Medal of Honor than any other job in the Navy. And, you know, that has to do with the fact that we are on the ground, fighting alongside Marines."

—Eric Gilmet, US Navy corpsman

Quoted in Nick Coffman, "Chief Eric Gilmet: A Spec Ops Lifesaver's Journey, Corpsman History, and His Toughest School," United American Patriots, December 7, 2020. www.uap.org.

the ability to transition back and forth between being a professional medical provider and a professional gun fighter all in the same day," explains one SARC. "It's definitely the adrenaline pumping. Looking at your own life and disregarding it to help everyone else around you."[18] SARCs serve in the field during combat and other missions and train with these types of scenarios when on bases.

Working Conditions

Most military medical personnel perform their jobs at hospitals and clinics on or near military bases, but they also perform their medical duties on ships, on airplanes, or in temporary spaces erected during exercises or actual missions Medical personnel who work on bases often have responsibilities that go beyond their specific assignments. Army veterinarian Breanna Johnson works in Fort Drum, New York, as the veterinary officer in charge. She describes her varied duties:

> I really love working with military dogs, that was my passion that was why I chose to get in [the military]. . . . But what you realize, once you get in, is I wear several hats. The veterinary corps officers are responsible for public health on posts, we also do a lot of food safety, so we inspect the food that goes to the food commissary to ensure that it's safe for the families that are purchasing it.[19]

FACT
The Navy Medical Corps is made up of forty-three hundred active-duty and reserve doctors who practice in twenty-three medical and surgical specialties.

Being in the medical field also means that you can be deployed to places of combat or in need of humanitarian aid. At these places, you may be working in temporary facilities and with fewer instruments and supplies than you would normally. Army physician Maria DeArman served in Afghanistan for a year as part of a mission to help the locals rebuild their country. The mission included clearing roads, helping build hospitals, and establishing health care. "I got to do women's health while I was there," DeArman explains. "Teach midwifery, how to deliver a baby, I got to [go on rounds] with Afghan doctors. It was a really cool opportunity for an entire year."[20]

An Army combat medic specialist sorts medical instruments for restocking. Medical personnel in the military include doctors, nurses, dentists, physical therapists, and others. They work in clinics, hospitals, and in the field.

Keeping the Air Force Mentally Healthy

"I'm currently a mental health element chief in our outpatient clinic at Joint Base Elmendorf-Richardson. I supervise thirty-eight staff members, providing twelve thousand appointments annually of mental health care to both our active-duty members as well as [their] beneficiaries. So, we provide outpatient care that consists of individual therapy, group therapy, as well as a variety of psychological testing, whether it's helping a flier overcome anxiety to fly an F-22 to helping a sniper calm down in their breathing and so they're able to accurately shoot the target as necessary. Ultimately, there's a variety of mental health techniques across the air force that are useful and beneficial for that success of that mission."

—Emanual Vondran, US Army psychologist

Quoted in U.S. Air Force Recruiting, *U.S. Air Force Clinical Psychologist*, YouTube, 2021. www.youtube.com/watch?v=wtR01UCplsM.

Finding a Good Fit

Being calm under pressure is necessary for all medical fields. Emergencies happen, and medical personnel must be able to deal with them without unnerving the patients. Providing services to people and/or animals in extreme situations—such as under fire in a war zone or on a helicopter tending to a wounded person being transported to a hospital—requires focus and resourcefulness.

Being able to communicate well and show empathy are also among the needed characteristics for working with patients who might be anxious, afraid, or in pain. "Nursing to me means providing quality, compassionate care to patients in their time of need, that they may not show you they need that care but it's something that can change a negative situation into a positive one,"[21] said Lena Fabian, an army certified nurse midwife at William Beaumont Army Medical Center at Fort Bliss in Texas. Fabian and others in the field know that how they deal with patients affects the successful outcome of the patients' overall care.

Job Prospects in the Civilian World

Skilled medical professionals in the military will find many opportunities in the civilian world—and most are on the high-paying end. Doctors, nurses, ophthalmologists, dentists, and the like are needed in the civilian world, and they can find jobs in hospitals, clinics, urgent care clinics, home health care, and more. For enlisted personnel, their medical background also allows an easier transition to civilian jobs due to their training and experience. Jobs open to those who served in enlisted roles include laboratory technicians, emergency services technicians, nurse's aides, certified nursing assistants, and more. All military medical personnel will have skills that are transferrable to a career in the civilian world.

CHAPTER FIVE

STEM Careers

STEM is of major importance in the military because so much of the world is reliant on engineering, science, and computer technology. The need for STEM personnel in the military continues to increase, especially with the establishment of the US Space Force in 2019. Most of the jobs in the space force are technology related. Personnel in this branch work in areas such as space systems, satellites, and antennas. Because the need is great, recruiters often visit high schools in hopes of generating interest among students for STEM jobs in the military.

Many STEM careers in the military are in the field of information technology, or IT. Computers are as ubiquitous in the military as they are in civilian life. Computer technology—including servers, databases, software, networks, and overall infrastructure—is essential to a functioning military, and people are needed to operate, install, repair, and maintain all of that technology. The job of an army IT specialist, for instance, involves the installation, maintenance, and testing of computer networks, hardware, and software. As one army IT technician explains, "An IT technician basically builds the communication infrastructure to facilitate the communication within the military. Everything we do will basically have a direct impact on whether our mission is accomplished."[22]

Other military STEM careers include all types of engineers, missile and space technologists, scientists, meteorologists, and sonar technicians. Engineers design and oversee construction and repair projects on bases and in the field throughout the world. While deployed to Afghanistan, army engineering officer James Kemter was in charge of building projects such as barracks, roads, and the headquarters for army and Afghan agencies. "Just seeing the quality of life of a really poor nation—third-world nation—get improved was something that made you really feel good. Be it building a road or getting a police station built in places they've never had a police station . . . just seeing the overall prosperity . . . start booming because you just turned a little goat trail into a road that a car can actually drive down,"[23] Kemter says of the satisfaction he gets from his job.

Education and Training

Engineering officers in the military must get a bachelor's degree before being commissioned as an officer. They can do this before entering the military or through a military program, such as the Reserve Officers' Training Corps, that funds their education in return for a specified number of years of service. Either way, once they obtain a degree, they attend training specific to their job.

FACT

As of July 2022 there were 1,634 officers in the US Navy's Civil Engineer Corps stationed at over 140 different locations across the world.

Officers entering as engineers will attend training specific to their job. As an example, an officer in the navy's Civil Engineer Corps will spend approximately four months in Port Hueneme, California, learning about subjects such as managing construction contracts, leading field construction, and overseeing public works on a base. Air force and army engineers attend an engineering leadership course for approximately nineteen weeks at Fort Leonard Wood in Missouri. In other STEM fields—for example, navy meteorologists and oceanography officers—training involves a five-week course at the Naval Information Warfare Training Group in Gulfport, Mississippi.

Putting in the Time

"Whenever . . . mail goes down or the internet goes down or just specific things that happen within the IT realm of stuff that we're in charge of—you've got to troubleshoot, you know dig into it, so that's the fun part. . . . I've put in a couple twenty-four-hour-plus days of troubleshooting. I mean that happened, it's not like common, but it happens sometimes."

—A US Navy information systems technician

Quoted in Shae Taylor, *Life as an IT in the Navy*, YouTube, September 9, 2021. www.youtube.com/watch?v=ojyehd-q5lo.

Enlisted personnel who want to enter any STEM-related career generally need high scores on the arithmetical reasoning and electronics portions of the ASVAB. Training for enlisted personnel in their specialties begins after boot camp, when they are sent for advanced training. As an example, a space systems operations specialist in the space force receives nine weeks of training at Vandenberg Air Force Base in California. Navy IT technicians train on Microsoft, Cisco, and Oracle software and hardware fundamentals for twenty-four weeks in Pensacola, Florida. Army satellite communication systems operator specialists are assigned to Fort Gordon in Georgia for their training. For this job, "advance training will begin . . . with satellite theory and usage. You'll continue with hands-on training in the inspection, troubleshooting, and preventive maintenance that will be a core function of your duties," explains an army promotional video. "Next the army will train you in multichannel satellite communication systems, including the installation, operation, and maintenance of the equipment that transmits and receives."[24] Whatever STEM field enlisted military personnel enter, they receive intense technical training and often gain certifications that are applicable in the civilian world.

On the Job

For many of the military personnel who work in STEM jobs, their workdays (and worknights) involve oversight of various systems, from command networks to satellites. Enlisted personnel typically handle the programming, testing, and overall operation of those systems. Officers manage staff and strategize on how to meet short- and long-term goals. Space force officer Amber Hagy is the commander of Company A at the Wideband Satellite Communications Operations Center at Fort Detrick in Maryland. Her company oversees the operation of twelve satellites. Their job is to monitor and control the satellites' locations and movements and make sure they continue to operate properly. The satellites provide military and government agencies access to the US Department of Defense's Defense Information System Network, which supports telecommunications on a global scale. Hagy says she encounters all sorts of challenges in her job—which is one of the things she likes about it. "Generally," she says, "there is a set schedule but that tends to go out the window. There's new challenges all the time, especially here. . . . I love puzzles to solve and there's always something new to

A Need for the Space Force

"GPS [Global Positioning System] satellites not only allow for a safe navigation for land, sea, and air, but they also provide support for financial transactions and protocols, and without this protocol support that's provided by these GPS satellites, it can cause a multitude of things. For example, it can cause internet to slow, it can cause access to the cloud to deteriorate, or for control systems for energy grid, or water or transportation it could begin to fail . . . so we need a branch of our military dedicated to its defense."

—Cindy Burkett, US Space Force officer

Quoted in Space Nerd Confessions, *Why We Need the US Space Force*, YouTube, 2023. www.youtube.com/watch?v=gnNEF5dsNVo.

Marines set up satellite communication equipment. Equipment of this type is used for detecting, locating, tracking, and engaging units at sea, in the air, on land, and in cyberspace.

troubleshoot with communications, whether it's here within our facility or overseas."[25]

Military members who work in IT positions oversee overall functioning of networks, hardware, software, and communications. A navy information systems technician stationed on a ship based in Yokosuka, Japan, describes the work he does on network and communication systems. "On a day-to-day basis," he says, "you're connecting transmitters, to transmit a signal, and receivers, which will receive your signal . . . you connect wires, the transmitter, and receiver and with whatever frequency that the navy gives us . . . then you connect them to a phone for people who work in our operations department . . . you are basically in control of the ship being capable of communicating."[26]

Working Conditions

Most IT work is done indoors in air-conditioned rooms to keep servers and other equipment cool. This holds true even for navy IT personnel who are stationed on ships or submarines. One

> **FACT**
> Meteorologists with the US Air Force Reserve's Fifty-Third Weather Reconnaissance Squadron serve as flight directors on flights into hurricanes and cyclones to obtain weather data.

disadvantage these IT professionals face is working in tight spaces and conditions that include low lighting.

Certain STEM jobs include some outdoor work. For example, engineers overseeing construction contracts and projects will likely visit those job sites as part of managing the project's progress. Others, such as cable and antennae specialists, may spend time outdoors checking on the condition of antennas or fiber-optic cable systems and repairing or replacing them. Air force weather specialists who work in combat operations are also likely to spend time outdoors working with ground troops as weather advisers.

Finding a Good Fit

STEM careers are for those who have an interest and ability in technical, scientific, and mathematics fields. Wanting to understand why things work the way they do is a key trait of anyone desirous of a STEM career. Knowledge of higher-level mathematics and the ability to learn and understand new material is also important in the STEM fields.

In the military, those in STEM need to excel at communication since they are often in situations in which they are briefing leaders, working to provide service to customers (both military and governmental), and writing technical briefings. Additionally, they generally need to work well with others because their jobs involve a great deal of teamwork. The ability to combine technical knowledge with an understanding of people will help those in these careers succeed.

Job Prospects in the Civilian World

Anyone who has worked in the STEM fields in the military will likely find many job opportunities in the civilian world. According to the Bureau of Labor Statistics, employment in computer and information technology occupations is projected to increase by 15 percent from now to 2031, faster than the average for all occupations. Types of IT jobs available are database administrators, network administrators, software developers, testers, and more. Engineering is another high-demand field. A background in engineering can lead to a wide array of civilian jobs. People with military experience in civil engineering, for instance, can find jobs as project managers at construction companies or facilities management jobs in a public works department. A background in electrical engineering can lead to a job as a design engineer in a power company or a lead electrical engineer in an automotive company. Service members who worked with telecommunications or satellite technology are also likely to find plenty of job opportunities in civilian life in satellite communications and telecommunication industries as technicians and quality control specialists. Coming out of the military with STEM experience and training may lead to a high-paying job using the skills gained during service.

CHAPTER SIX

Mission Critical Careers

All military personnel—whether they work in a medical clinic, a supply depot, or a computer center—are trained to fight in a war, but for many, fighting is not their primary job. Together they perform a whole host of jobs that enable the military to carry out its various missions—during times of peace and times of war. They are joined, in every branch of the military, by personnel whose jobs are tied specifically to weaponry, combat, and the waging of war. These are the mission critical careers.

The navy's ships and submarines provide a naval presence in the world. Surface warfare officers control the ships' movements and weapons during exercises and actual missions. Enlisted personnel maintain and run the weapons systems.

Air operations are provided by the army, navy, and air force, with many different types of aircraft. From helicopters to fighter jets, pilots and their crews are needed to operate weapons systems and perform any electronic reconnaissance that is part of the mission. "It's an absolute blast. It's kind of a combination of being a NASCAR driver and playing a video game at the same time,"[27] is how air force F-35 fighter pilot Chris Shannon describes his job.

Mission critical jobs in the marine corps and army are mostly on land. These jobs are held by infantry officers and infantry enlisted personnel. They are trained to strategize and fight against the enemy on land. Army infantryman Mico Madera explains, "Our mission is to shoot, move, close with, and destroy the enemy."[28] Additionally, there are special operations units in all of the branches, from US Navy Sea, Air, and Land (SEAL) forces to US Army Rangers. They are specially trained in areas such as scuba diving, weaponry, and hand-to-hand combat. They conduct raids, engage the enemy in close combat, conduct reconnaissance, and complete stealth missions. All mission critical careers provide excitement, danger, and a chance to challenge oneself to perform skilled jobs under pressure.

Education and Training

The requirements for mission critical careers are rigorous for most of the jobs. As an example, pilots must have perfect vision. Infantrymen, SEALs, US Army Rangers, and other special forces must pass high-level physical tests to enter. In addition to physical tests, explosive ordnance disposal (EOD) personnel in the navy must pass a hyperbaric pressure tolerance test, while air force EODs must show they do not have claustrophobia.

The training for these jobs is hands-on and intensive. Navy, army, and air force pilots attend training for up to two years, depending on which aircraft they are learning to pilot. Navy pilots first attend a six-week air indoctrination course at the Naval Aviation Schools Command in Pensacola, Florida. From there, prospective helicopter pilots, fixed-wing pilots, and fighter pilots attend their specific training. The final phase is then advanced naval flight training, focusing on flying for missions. Enlisted personnel who serve on aircraft, such as operators who attack enemy submarines from the air, attend schools specific to their roles. As an example, navy air crew personnel attend Naval Aircrew Candidate School for eleven weeks in Pensacola, Florida, for training in aircrew duties, water rescue tactics, search and rescue, and land survival and safety.

FACT
The F-35 Lightning II has a top speed of Mach 1.6 (1,200 miles per hour) and is used by the US Marine Corps, US Air Force, and US Navy.

Navy SEALs, both officers and enlisted personnel, go through extreme training that pushes them mentally, emotionally, and physically. Extreme physical tests involving swimming in oceans, running miles with heavy gear in the desert, going for extended periods without sleep, and scuba diving tests are just a part of the course. Nearly 75 percent of the personnel who attempt the program do not make it through to the end. The other branches' special operations personnel go through similar training.

Surface warfare officers in the navy learn to pilot ships at Newport, Rhode Island. As a navy surface warfare officer on the USS *Chafee*, Kathryn Kirkwood gives steering and engine orders, or cons the ship, while standing watches on the ship's bridge. She attributes her success in this role to her training. She recalls one

An Air Force F-16 Fighting Falcon pilot inspects the aircraft's controls before a training flight. Every branch of the military includes personnel whose jobs are tied specifically to weaponry, combat, and the waging of war.

Facing Danger

"There's been times when I was standing over something that could kill me, and I was there trying to picture all the choices I made in life that got me to that moment."

—Carlos Villarreal, US Marine EOD technician

Quoted in Ryan Pickrell, "These Marines Do One of the Military's Most Dangerous Jobs," Business Insider, November 11, 2021. www.businessinsider.com.

of the first times she stood watch on a ship that was maneuvering out of port at Naval Station Pearl Harbor in Hawaii. "I was on bridge as watch stander with the navigator and it was a full power run, so we were going max speed. It was really incredible going as fast as we were in crossing situations and feeling totally confident in the situation and understanding what maneuvers we needed to make to remain safe."[29]

Infantry personnel also undergo rigorous physical and weapons training for the army and the marines. Marines attend a fifty-nine-day Infantry Training Battalion course. They learn, among other things, marksmanship, patrolling, grenade usage, and identifying and countering improvised explosive devices. As with all of these careers, the training is meant to prepare them for real-life missions in the military.

On the Job

Even when not on an actual mission, there are training exercises and constant preparation for those in mission critical jobs. Miguel Estrada, a gunner's mate on the navy destroyer USS *O'Kane*, has the job of overseeing a team that maintains and operates the destroyer's 5-inch (12.7 cm) Mark 45 lightweight gun, which looks like a cannon. The gun is designed for use against surface warships, for antiaircraft, and for shore bombardment to support amphibious operations. "The whole purpose behind

Honing Infantry Skills

"One of the fun events I've had in the army was going to NTC, the National Training Center, where we would have operations against a fake enemy, OPFOR. We'd fight them, we'd go to different towns, we'd move out to different areas and attack the enemy. And at the end of that, the mortars did a live fire, shot at least 500 rounds of different types of ammunition, and it was just fun to do our job."

—William Godwin, US Army indirect fire infantryman

Quoted in GoArmy, *Infantry Jobs in the Army*, YouTube, 2022. www.youtube.com/watch?v=fW-CRyHKTuE.

the [exercises] is to make sure our equipment operates how it is supposed to, effectively, and ensuring that our watch team know their positions and how to operate their equipment,"[30] Estrada explains. Throughout the days, his team also conducts damage-control drills in case a fire breaks out. He explains that drills are a major part of what they do, to be prepared for any event of fire or casualty.

Those who work in mission critical jobs understand that, at some point, they may find themselves in combat situations and in direct danger from enemy forces. In August 2021 air force pilot Braden Coleman, a C-17 large transport pilot, was deployed to Afghanistan as the United States was ending operations there. He was part of the last crew to transport Afghans and US troops out of the country. Conditions on the ground were extremely dangerous. As US aircraft took off, gunfire could be heard nearby, Taliban fighters were in sight, there was no rocket defense system to protect them, and there was no one in the airport control center to direct them out. Despite the dangers, he and other pilots worked together and relied on their training. "To see everybody, step up to make this happen in the amount of time that it took to happen, to move 124,000 people out in less than three weeks. I mean, I couldn't be prouder to be a C-17 pilot today,"[31] says Coleman. While there were casualties during the American exit, the pilots were able to get thousands to safety.

Working Conditions

Personnel in mission critical careers work in many different settings. Those in infantry, both enlisted personnel and officers, often work and train in areas from the desert to the Arctic. During training exercises and in real combat, they typically work outdoors and sleep in tents. The same is true for special operations forces. They are trained to operate in mountainous terrain, deserts, and jungles—basically, anywhere their particular skills and talents are needed. Other mission-centered personnel live and work on ships and submarines—sometimes spending six months or more aboard these vessels, sharing sleeping areas with others, and standing watches outside of their normal duties. In between ship and submarine duty stations, they may have assignments on base, planning strategy, tactics, and doing related jobs. Pilots, whether on base or on an aircraft carrier or amphibious assault ship, spend many hours—sometimes during the day, other times at night—practicing takeoffs, landings, and other maneuvers. For all, exercises day and night are a part of their jobs to keep them mission ready.

FACT
Infantry personnel make up 15 to 17 percent of the US Army.

Finding a Good Fit

Military personnel who work in mission critical jobs must be able to adapt to unexpected and challenging situations. They need to be quick-thinking and calm under pressure.

A high level of physical fitness is essential in any of these jobs. In some of the jobs, special physical skills, such as being a strong swimmer, are also necessary. The ability to read a map and having basic mechanical skills are also important. And, although being able to follow orders is essential in all areas of the military, it is especially crucial for those who work in mission-oriented jobs.

Job Prospects in the Civilian World

Mission critical jobs in the military can develop skills that will also be valuable in the civilian world. Leadership experience and expertise with weapons and weapons systems can lead to careers in the federal government or with defense contractors that provide support to the military. Infantry (enlisted) and those in special forces are often able to find careers in security, investigative work, and policing work. Pilots are able to find equivalent jobs in the civilian world, with many choosing to work for airlines or air freight companies or, if they flew helicopters, for medevac businesses. For all who serve, the lessons they learn in stressful and dangerous situations help them achieve success in any high-pressured career.

SOURCE NOTES

Introduction: Something for Everyone

1. Quoted in *First Black Female Fighter Pilot of U.S. Navy: Lt. j.g. Madeline Swegle*, YouTube, 2021. www.youtube.com/watch?v=9mjA-mDGLUU.
2. Aleda Leaks, *How Joining the Army Changed My Life*, YouTube, 2021. www.youtube.com/watch?v=ABplM3cDw7k.
3. Davis Jkwon, *Why You Should Join the Army*, YouTube, 2019. www.youtube.com/watch?v=L0Jo06Uwxeg.

Chapter One: Skilled Trades Careers

4. Quoted in DVIDS, "USS *Charleston* (LCS 18) Sailor in the Spotlight—Aviation Machinist's Mate Airman Elisa Morales," May 24, 2021. www.dvidshub.net.
5. Quoted in Mya Crosby, "HVAC Keeps It Cool," DVIDS, April 12, 2019. www.dvidshub.net.
6. Quoted in America's Navy, *Navy Machinists Mate Nuclear*, YouTube, 2019. www.youtube.com/watch?v=dGoiVaMd_50.
7. Quoted in Courtney Pollock, "Leading from the Front: MRCS Tarah Horney," DVIDS, March 22, 2019. www.dvidshub.net.

Chapter Two: Service Careers

8. Quoted Porsha Thompson, "Cooking with Heart," DVIDS, September 23, 2022. www.dvidshub.net.
9. Quoted in Ariana Torman, "NMCP Top Supply Officer's Impactful Pandemic Efforts," DVIDS, October 9, 2020. www.dvidshub.net.
10. Quoted in Everyday Chaplain, *A Day in the Life of a Chaplain*, YouTube, 2021. www.youtube.com/watch?v=lr5ktRZUHc0.
11. Quoted in Torman, "NMCP Top Supply Officer's Impactful Pandemic Efforts."

Chapter Three: Intelligence and Cybersecurity Careers

12. Quoted in DVIDS, "Cyber Snapshot: Spc. Steffan Hinkle," February 4, 2020. www.dvidshub.net.
13. Quoted in Real Sailors Real Sea Stories, *Navy Intelligence Specialist with IS1 Shears*, YouTube, 2021. www.youtube.com/watch?v=Vx22BMvuwhE&t=540s.
14. Quoted in US Military Moments, *Faces of the Defender: Cyber Surety (2019)*, YouTube, 2019. www.youtube.com/watch?v=NBZPCe3eWs0.
15. Quoted in CommissionED, *14N Intelligence Officer*, YouTube, 2022. www.youtube.com/watch?v=C-LR6HJY7Uw.

Chapter Four: Medical Careers

16. Quoted in Marcy Sanchez, "Pharmacy Instrumental During Pandemic, Recognized During Pharmacy Week," DVIDS, October 16, 2020. www.dvidshub.net.
17. Quoted in GoArmy, *What Is an Army Radiology Specialist?*, YouTube, 2022. www.youtube.com/watch?v=fJ7EqltubPA.
18. Quoted in America's Navy, *Navy Special Amphibious Reconnaissance Corpsman—SARC*, YouTube, 2019. www.youtube.com/watch?v=5ONl8Z1s-Ac.
19. Quoted in Today's Military, "Veterinarians," 2023. www.todaysmilitary.com.
20. Quoted in Today's Military, "Maria DeArman," July 29, 2021. www.todaysmilitary.com.
21. Quoted in Marcy Sanchez, "WBAMC Nurses Recognized for Care, Compassion," DVIDS, November 26, 2018. www.dvidshub.net.

Chapter Five: STEM Careers

22. Quoted in US Army Recruiting, *MOS 25B Information Technology Specialist*, YouTube, 2021. www.youtube.com/watch?v=EuLL7Cjrv0M.
23. Quoted in Today's Military, "James Kemter," 2023. www.todaysmilitary.com.

24. GoArmy Kansas City, *Army MOS 25S Satellite Communications Systems Operator Maintainer*, YouTube, 2020. www.youtube.com/watch?v=3EpuoiprHtM.
25. Quoted in Aaron Rognstad, "Profiles in Space: Commander of Communication," DVIDS, October 19, 2020. www.dvidshub.net.
26. Quoted in Shae Taylor, *Life as an IT in the Navy*, YouTube, September 9, 2021. www.youtube.com/watch?v=ojyehd-q5lo.

Chapter Six: Mission Critical Careers

27. Quoted in Fox 13 News Utah, *Day in the Life of a F-35 Pilot*, YouTube, 2022. www.youtube.com/watch?v=kkm64XQOJrM.
28. Quoted in Today's Military, "Infantry Officers," 2022. www.todaysmilitary.com.
29. Quoted in Surface Warriors, *SWO Pipeline ENS Kirkwood*, YouTube, 2021. www.youtube.com/watch?v=nG-H52V5pQg.
30. Quoted in Forbes Breaking News, "US Navy Reveals What Daily Life Is Like for a Gunner's Mate on Destroyer USS *O'Kane*," YouTube, 2022. www.youtube.com/watch?v=mECw2myzz64.
31. Quoted in Lolita Baldor, "'It Looked Apocalyptic': Crew Describes Afghan Departure," AP News, September 21, 2021. https://apnews.com.

FIND OUT MORE

Bureau of Labor Statistics

www.bls.gov/ooh/military/military-careers.htm

The Bureau of Labor Statistics, a government agency, measures labor market activity, working conditions, and salaries, with this info on its website. The military section on the website provides military career information.

Military.com

www.military.com

Military veterans, active-duty military, and anyone interested in the military can find news and military information on this site. It contains information on specific jobs, wages, how to join the military, and more to assist those considering the military.

Today's Military

www.todaysmilitary.com

The US Department of Defense provides this website. It provides information regarding enlisted and officer career opportunities.

US Air Force

www.airforce.com

This is the official website of the US Air Force. The careers section provides information on a variety of careers organized by areas of interest.

US Army

www.army.mil

This is the official website of the US Army. The section regarding careers provides information on the different types of careers, how to join, and pay and benefits.

US Coast Guard

www.uscg.mil

This is the official website of the US Coast Guard. In the career section, one can find information on available careers based on interest.

US Marine Corps

www.marines.com

This is the official website of the US Marine Corps. It includes a section on roles in the US Marine Corps, describing the different career paths possible.

US Navy

www.navy.com

This is the US Navy's recruiting website. One can find information on available careers, pay and benefits, and requirements to join.

US Space Force

www.spaceforce.mil

This is the official website of the US Space Force. In the career section, information regarding both officer and enlisted careers in this branch is available.

INTERVIEW WITH AN ARMY NATIONAL GUARD FIREFIGHTER

Scott Frischer served as a firefighter in the Army National Guard from 2006 to 2019, achieving the level of station chief while stationed at Joint Base Cape Cod. He now works as a firefighter in Massachusetts. He answered questions about his career by email.

Q: Why and how did you join the National Guard?
A: I joined the National Guard while in between jobs. I was trying to find a full-time job on a fire department and was working on getting all the required certifications. A friend of mine who was already in the National Guard was transferring to an Army firefighting unit and asked me to think about the idea of joining to do so as well. I figured it would be a great opportunity to get all the required certifications, training, and some experience to help me acquire a civilian job.

Q: Which training did you have or get for this career?
A: Soldiers beginning their initial training to become Army Firefighters are sent to the Department of Defense fire academy. After completing this 16-week academy, you will be nationally certified in the firefighter 1 and 2 level, Airport rescue firefighter, and Hazardous materials operation level. After graduation, you will be sent back to your unit for additional training and certification courses. Some of these would include driver/operator, fire officer, fire instructor, fire inspector. All are also nationally recognized certifications.

Q: How would you describe a typical workday?
A: A typical workday would vary on our unit's status. While on a weekend drill status we would start the day with unit physical training, then typically training would be conducted for the

remainder of the day. This training would cover Firefighter tasks and skills as well as the ones of the Soldier, all need to be covered within a training year. While on mission, the start of the day would bring equipment check. A functions check would be performed on all carried and mission critical equipment to confirm readiness. After that, a reduced amount of training would be conducted in a way that would maintain readiness and the ability to respond if needed.

Q: What did you like most about the job?
A: That everything that I trained in helped me in my civilian firefighter position. Every certification I obtained is nationally recognized in the civilian fire service. I went into the National Guard looking to acquire skills that would help me in the civilian world, and I feel that is what I did.

Q: What did you like least about the job?
A: The time commitment is a lot. The training schedule is usually full to keep up with all the required annual tasks and skills that the Army firefighter has to be proficient in, this is in addition to the training requirements of the Soldier. I missed a lot while I was in, and I will never get that time back with my family.

Q: What were your most interesting duty stations or deployments and why?
A: I was assigned to small a group of Army Firefighters that was sent to Paraguay on a training mission. This was to meet with a unit of their Airforce Firefighters and exchange training techniques and equipment used to respond to and handle a variety of emergency situations. I really enjoyed the opportunity to be part of this cross training, the experience was a once in a lifetime one.

Q: What personal qualities do you find the most valuable for this type of work?
A: Reliable, self-motivated, hardworking, caring, patient, and a strong willingness to learn are some qualities I think are valuable.

Q: What advice do you have for students who might be interested in this military career?

A: This is a rewarding career field that you can advance in during your time in the Military. This is also one of the fields that you can bring everything you've earned and learned with you into the civilian equivalent position. If this is what you want to do, take advantage of every class, course, and training opportunity that is offered to you.

A SAMPLING OF JOBS IN THE MILITARY

Air force navigators
Animal care specialist
Aviation survival technician
Avionics electrical technician
Boatswain's mate
Cannon crewmember
Chemical, biological, radiological, and nuclear officer
Cryptologic digital network tech
Cryptologic technician interpretive
Defense artillery officer
Dietician
Diver
Engineering aide
Fire control specialist
Horizontal construction engineer
Joint fire support specialist
Logistics officer
Logistics specialist
Musician
Navy diver
Operations specialist
Ordnance specialist
Pararescueman
Quartermaster
Religious program specialist
Sere specialist
Squadron ordnance technician
Tactical aircraft maintenance
Torpedoman's mate
Transportation officer
Weapons administrator

Editor's note: The online *Occupational Outlook Handbook* of the US Department of Labor's Bureau of Labor Statistics is an excellent source of information on jobs in hundreds of career fields, including many of those listed here. The *Occupational Outlook Handbook* may be accessed online at www.bls.gov/ooh.

INDEX

Note: Boldface page numbers indicate illustrations.

PICTURE CREDITS

Cover: Marine Corps Sgt. Israel Chincio (top left); Air Force Airman Eduardo Figueroa (top right); Navy Petty Officer 2nd Class Michael Chen (bottom left); Navy Petty Officer 2nd Class Juan Sua (bottom right)

6: Maury Aaseng
10: Cameron Porter, Army
18: Navy Mass Communication Specialist Seaman Jose Madriga
24: Space Force Tech. Sgt. Luke Kitterman
32: Army Spc. Preston Robinson
39: Marine Corps Cpl. Samuel Fletcher
44: Air Force Senior Airman Brooke Moeder

ABOUT THE AUTHOR

Leanne Currie-McGhee lives in Norfolk, Virginia, with her husband, Keith, children, Grace and Sol, and dog, Delilah. She served as a Civil Engineer Corps officer in the US Navy prior to embarking on a career of writing educational books.